Mother Ayahuasca

Amazon

I'm not sure how I ended up here.

Animals, everywhere. Birds, bees. Mosquitos. Another bite.

Another one bites the dust.

A string of events led me to Cusco, Peru. After five months in Cusco, I travel to Iquitos. Amazon jungle. Rain forest. Wood. Jungle.

Death.

Ayahuasca.

A rebirth.

Recovery.

And so it is.

Friday night

One more time. I'm going in.

The temple, maloka.

I did not eat tonight.

I feel empty, terrified.

There's no light. Only jungle sounds, animals, frogs. Birds.

Cats.

Eyes

The night is black. Like ink, dripping off my forehead. I'm hot. I feel sick. I run to the bathroom before we start.

Am I truly going to do this?

Yes.

God bless.

Mother

Mother Ayahuasca. I devote this ceremony to you. May I find peace in your arms. May I breathe through your waves of light, energy, visions, truth. Imagination.

I'm not sure what's real, no more.

When I close my eyes, I see everything. Anything. Images, lines, forms. Dust. Forms change size, pattern, color.

It's endless.

Why am I here? Why do I do what I do? Will I feel better, soon?

I might.

I do not feel better, yet.

A precious child of God

I pray.

Ho'oponopono.

"I'm sorry. Please forgive me, I love you. Thank you".

I pray for my mom, for Mike who got carried out of the temple, a few minutes earlier. I pray for myself.

My family, friends.

I pray for everyone.

If I make it out of here alive, I pray, I will be a child of God.

A precious child of God.

Surrender

May I forgive, myself, others, for past harm, heartbroken, moments. May I forgive everyone, myself included.

May I come clean. Purge, pray, wash off what's no longer serving me. May I surrender to you, Mother Earth, Pachamama.

Peace.

Out.

Food

We eat lightly.

Fruits for breakfast, rice, eggs. I'm no longer vegan, for now. Beans for lunch, rice.

Rest.

Recovery.

We do not use oil, salt, sugar, spice.

Clean.

We cook simple. A dieta.

Plant-based, whole-hearted. Prepared by Mamitas in the jungle.

And so there's love. In everything we do, eat, say, see. There's love. Love for nature, plants, animals, air.

Respect.

Reverence.

A humble feeling towards all elements of nature. Sun, sea, salt, rain, air, earth. Fire. Dust.

Stone.

Sink

Serenity.

A ceremony.

Cult.

World

Here's what's true.

For years, I've been living in a world way scarier than Ayahuasca.

A world in which fear, governs, love, fades, quickly.

Now, I'm opening up every vessel of my single Self. My heart.

Art.

Father

"Use your common sense", my father said, in my vision.

"Use your common sense. Be calm, just breathe. This will be over soon".

I'm calm. I breathe.

It is, over soon.

We

Later that day I sit, wait, wonder.

I see others, myself. All of us.

Different but similar. Similar but not the same.

We're all just, a different version of each other.

Mother.

Earth.

Wednesday

Here's what's different. I feel sane.

No longer sick, sorry. But strong, solid. Sane.

I've seen Spirit, saints. Fantasy figures. Female heroes. Fiction stories. My father. God. Telling me to calm down, let go, set free. Go out, just be.

Free.

Stay

It's all good. It's all fine. It's okay.

Stay.

Holiday

When we're not drinking, Ayahuasca, it's almost as if we're on a holiday. Summer camp.

We play, go out. Swimming, fishing. Cayman hunt.

We go out, daily, to visit other communities.

Only I didn't.

I got bitten so bad by the time we arrived, I needed to return home.

Ohm.

Arkana Spiritual Center.

And so it is.

Fish

But it's not. A holiday.

It's a retreat.

We wake up early for breakfast. After breakfast, we gather in the maloka to share, stories, tell, truth. Experience.

Some of us tell amusing tales, others frightening stories. It's always different. Every day.

The medicine works differently for all of us.

There is no line.

Lines gets blurry. Grey, green. Colors, fade. Away, get ready. For another wave of emotions, music. Art.

From the heart.

There's three shamans guiding the ceremony. Night after night, they sing. Songs. Icarus.

Limpiame, curame, cuerposito.

Before ceremony, we bath in flowers. We wash off what's left, of the day. Entering a new era, night.

Fight.

Abuelita

They say the plant will do the work for you. It gives you what you need, not what you want. It shows you, the way.

Stay.

One

And we connect. In ceremony, over breakfast. Another story.

I recognize myself in every single one of us.

A stripper, banker. A singer-songwriter, athlete. A war veteran. A mother of four. An injured young man hoping for recovery. An addict. Heroin, steroids. Amphetamines, Adderall. Alcohol.

Alright.

Night.

Key

In life, we unlearn.

Doing, seeing.

Being.

Freeing

Oneself. Others.

Art.

Mothers

Memories.

My birth. Yours.

Our birth. When will be finally free?

Together. To gather. It is so much fun, to just be.

See. Life.

Strive.

Say what? Say sorry.

Often. Times.

Surrender

/səˈrɛndə/

stop resisting to an enemy or opponent and submit to their authority.
"over 140 rebels surrendered to the authorities"

give up or hand over (a person, right, or possession), typically on compulsion or demand.
"in 1815 Denmark surrendered Norway to Sweden"

Story

I give up.

Controlling, manipulating. Life. Or so I think. Try. Do it right. Fight. Give up.

Let go, let go. They say, let God.

Decide.

Fantasy

In hindsight, we do not remember. The struggle.

Fight.

We only see, the success. Story.

The bigger picture. Frame.

It's like giving birth. Over and over and over again. There's nothing left to be afraid of. Anymore.

No more. Fear. Excuses. Fairy.

Tales.

No more lullabies. Songs. Sacrifices.

I just am.

Me.

Free

And so I write. A book.

I tell. My story.

Glory.

Hallelujah

Come.

Clean.

Celtic

Woman.

"Amazing Grace, How sweet the sound
That saved a wretch like me
I once was lost, but now am found
T'was blind but now I see
T'was Grace that taught my heart to fear
And Grace, my fears relieved
How precious did that grace appear
The hour I first believed
Through many dangers, toils and snares
We have already come.
T'was grace that brought us safe thus far
And grace will lead us home,
And grace will lead us home
Amazing grace, Howe Sweet the sound
That saved a wretch like me
I once was lost but now am found
T'was blind but now I see
Was blind, but now I see"

Few days earlier

When Mother Ayahuasca calls, you know, you must listen. There is simply no other way.

And so I fly from Lima to Iquitos, Peru.

I check dates, flights, bus, tickets.

It's not an accident, I'm flying today. I lost my first child, few years ago, in May.

Earth

Little by little I understand more about my journey. But not yet now.

It's still too raw.

Fresh, familiar.

Feminine.

Little by little I will know where to go. What I'm here for.

Planet Earth.

An illusion.

Life

In ceremony, ordinary life does no longer exist. I do no longer exist. I'm everyone, everything at the same time.

I change form, shape, color. Snakes.

I see angels, God.

Universal connection. Connectivity. Issues.

I try to make sense of it all but I can't, do so. I'm someone different. I no longer see straight, lines, lullabies. I surrender.

And set free.

Fall.

Fear

A massive reset. That's what I need.

Do I?

If you believe so, you do.

A new future. Family. Possible scenario. For life.

Clarity.

Insight.

It's all just projection. Images. Mind.

It's no longer true.

And you, how do you do?

Lost

If I lose it, I might find it as well.

Ayahuasca

A journey. A flight. A discovery.

Channel.

Arrival

When all is said and done you will wake up.

You will be fine.

You will be better than ever before.

You will come clean.

And so it is.

Jose

I text Jose. "I'm in".

What's your best price?

I will surrender.

Bend.

Become a human being.

No longer doing but being.

Seeing, saying.

Truth.

Care

The less I care for others, the more they care for me.

I've been doing way too much for way too long.

For others.

Mothers.

Power

It is time now, to live for me.

Free.

Peru

I need to learn how to draw lines. Boundaries.

Protect myself better. From negativity, others. Draining me.

If I'm not helping myself, I'm helping others.

I'd love some free time too.

Air

Few days later I'm on a plane. I stop by my brother in Lima. We say hi. We're no longer family, but friends.

Different but similar.

Similar but not the same.

Spirit birds.

Eagle

When I wake up there's still few of us left.

I slept a long night. Full of dreams, American stories. A vintage market. Friends. A boyfriend. Girl. Friend.

We fell in love in my hometown.

Vivid dreams of what could be. Me, my future, life. Love.

Life, as we live it and love, as we imagine it to be. Free.

Someone said, "you fall in love with a soul, not a body. Gender. Sex".

You fall in love with a Soul.

It's true.

And so do you.

Parents

I'm not sure if my parents were ever in love.

They were, at the start, but then they lost, their love quickly.

Fights. Children. Stories.

They play pretend. Love. They cooperate in life.

They're mutually exclusive.

They work, play, art. Travel, trips. Pictures, stories. But I'm not sure, if they're still, in love.

They do not kiss, touch.

They talk. At times, when my father's brave enough to listen.

Usually, he's not. He's elsewhere.

Ayahuasca.

Childhood

Memories.

Apologies.

Pictures.

Images of what was, my life.

Oslo. Travel, trips. Things to do.

A list.

Norway.

Art, museum. Cold.

News.

War.

There's war everywhere in the world.

A waiting list.

When is it my time to come?

Home

My home is in Cusco, for now.

Only I'm not there yet. I'm still here.

Amazon, story. I write.

Ayahuasca.

Morning

A baby cries.

Bug, bees. A hen.

Early morning.

Law firm. Life. For years, I drove to work, every day.

Office. Life. A desk. Coffee.

Salad for lunch, my boss. Expecting more of me, every day. I pray.

For him, others. I pray for everyone.

May you be happy, may you be calm. May you live with ease.

I pray for myself, as well.

I'm sorry. Please forgive me. I love you.

Thank you.

Students

Memories.

My students.

I lived a beautiful life.

Gratefulness.

Bird

Why do we fly so far from where we belong?

Free

Another friend.

A wedding.

I'm single.

I'm single surrounded by couples.

Two.

I'm one.

And you, how do you do?

Lonely

There was a time where I wanted to come home but I couldn't.

My parents didn't let me, come home.

They sent me away.

Now, I stay.

Sponsor

"What would love do", Harriet would ask.

"Stay", I would reply.

I would love to stay here a little bit longer.

I would love to write my first book.

"So stay", she would say.

Harriet is right.

Most of the time. Teo too.

My Tao is Teo.

And so it is.

12 Steps

London, my second home.

First home, lately. Before I moved here.

I work my steps.

Step five, to be precise. It's not easy. I'm so far, away, from home.

From London.

My home-base.

Homerun.

Another story.

London

I love London.

I spent quite some time in London.

Quite some time.

Some quiet time.

And so it is.

Geographicals

Overseas, shore.

London.

Rain.

"Nothing heals me like you do"

I got lost, often in London.

I always found my way, home.

Friends. Coach. Fashion. Model. Jim. Father. Fellowship.

My fellowship saved my life.

Anonymous

I went to meetings every day.

My fellowship.

Art.

My sponsor. Harriet.

The best.

"Just surrender", she'd say.

Surrender.

This is not, a test.

God will do, the rest.

Cold

I wake up. Another day.

I take a shower, cold. I sweat. My palms, dry. My body, hot.

I did not drink last night.

Fresh.

Saturday

I pray.

God, where do I go next?

                             Journey

I stay few more days in the Amazon.

I'm not sure how long, yet.

I did not book a flight home, yet.

I'm here.

Queer

I'm here and I've never felt better before.

Boat

"The Red Turtle".

A movie.

I did not see the end, yet.

It's a sad story.

In a beautiful setting.

An island.

Song

"Our love was lost
But now we've found it
Our love was lost
And hope was gone
Our love was lost
But now we've found it
And if you flash your heart
I won't deny it
I promise
I promise
Your walls are up
Too cold to touch it
Your walls are up
Too high to climb
I know it's hard
But I can still hear it beating
So if you flash your heart
I won't mistreat it
I promise
I promise"

The Temper Trap, Love Lost

Life

Another song.

Will it ever end?

Aretha

"Respect".

A biography.

Written by David Ritz.

Other people shower. I want to shower.

Is it too late to shower?

Move

I must move. Action. A new day.

Stay.

Marriage

Teo texts me.

"Sofia, do you remember the name of the restaurant we went to in Paris"?

We went to Paris for my birthday. One day.

We fought plenty.

The past is no longer the present moment.

There's so much past.

It does not matter no more.

What matters most, is now.

This moment. Today.

And so I stay.

Women

At home, I participated in plenty of women's circles.

A womb healing. Meditation. Art.

A mood board. Coaching.

Stories.

"We, women. We grow strong, together".

Flexible, strong.

Beautiful.

"I am beautiful, I am bountiful, I am bliss".

I give birth.

Another story.

Buried in my body, my muscles. My heart.

Where do I start?

Heart

I got pregnant twice.

Once when I was younger, once when I was older. By accident.

"How can that happen", you may say.

"I don't know", I would reply.

Love finds a way. Always.

My baby found a way. Into my belly, breasts, womb.

Uterus.

I wasn't ready yet.

I was ready but I didn't know so yet.

I was terrified.

Of giving, what I never received.

Love.

Art. Belonging.

Truth.

A boy.

He's doing fine. He left my body in time.

A girl.

She's still with me.

"Momma", she says, "your time is now".

Do not wait, apologize, pretend. Live your life. Fully.

Your time is now.

The Beatles

"All you need is love, all you need is love
All you need is love, love, love is all you need

All you need is love
All you need is love, love, love is all you need

There's nothing you can know that isn't known
Nothing you can see that isn't shown
There's nowhere you can be that isn't where you're meant to be
It's easy"

Love

One shower later.

I feel better.

Fresh.

Perfume

Stay.

Water

I shower few times a day.

Amazon water.

It's no waste.

Energy

It's all energy.

People connect, greet, tell, stories.

Over breakfast.

Last day.

The retreat is almost over.

One more meeting.

Group share.

"Sharing is caring", they say.

It's okay.

Road

I finish packing.

It's not much.

A sweater, two, pants, T-shirts. Mosquito spray.

Why don't I stay?

Avión.

My flight takes off.

Heart

If only I'd be brave enough to listen.

To my heart.

I'd love to stay. Here.

A little bit longer.

Stronger.

Surrender

Pray

Why is it so difficult to practice what I preach?

Cusco

Ohm

I'm not sure why I'm here. Everything feels different. I'm different.

I want to continue, my journey. Amazon. A warrior. Into the woods, world, alive.

Awake.

I want to continue exploring what's next. The present moment. Future.

Alive.

I'll join my writer's group on Thursday. Return to recovery on Monday. Make up my mind on Tuesday.

Coffee

I feel plenty.

I no longer want to live, in Cusco.

I'd like to move to Sacred Valley. Soon.

Air, woods, wild, life. Plants.

People.

Play

There's too much going on in Cusco. Coffee, bars, candy, shops. Tourism.

Expensive restaurants.

It is time to make a change.

Again.

Amen

Brothers, sisters. We unite.

In the name of love.

And so it is.

Rain

Endless amounts of rain drip of my shoulders, chest.

A raincoat.

I let go.

I let be.

My hopes, plans for the future. For now, I revert to daily life society.

Why? Commitment. Responsibility. Art.

From the heart.

Does it matter?

Yes.

Chess

You do not need to play, pretend, no more.

You can just, be.

Free.

Demons

At night, I see demons. Telling me what I did not know before.

Or did I?

How difficult it is to put myself first.

How different my life will be once I do, put, myself first.

I'm not going crazy. I'm just living life. Change. Love. Heart. Break.

I'm just living life.

Love.

Another story.

Help

When I'm not helping myself, I'm helping others.

By helping others, I help myself.

I teach my classes.

I take my time.

I wake up early, do my best.

Is this life?

No, it's not.

There's more to it than this.

There must be more to it than this.

And so it is.

Lisa

A novel.

"Doves Fly In My Heart".

Amazon

Story

I miss my flight. Home.

I did not miss my flight. It's a conscious decision. I decide to stay a little bit longer, here.

There.

Ohm

Iquitos

We're 10.

Denise, John. Joachim, Erin. Bryan, Myriam. Bill, Heidi. Hallelujah.

We're plenty.

Michele.

Mike.

Who else did I forget?

Jungle

We swim, drink, go out.

We don't.

I don't.

I do drink.

A margarita.

I miss my mom.

When I miss my mom, I drink a margarita. Or I eat a margarita pizza.

It's a bad habit.

It's her habit.

The drinking. Not the pizza.

Her name is Margareta.

And so I copy what I've learned, so far.

Sober

I decide here and now that I'll be sober for the next 30 days.

A month.

Amen.

I've done this before.

I've been sober forever.

Spirits interfere with Spirit.

God.

My guides within.

And so it is.

Night

At night I wake up, alive.

It's 4:44.

The lights are on in the hallway. Hotel.

La Casona.

I take my computer, write. Get some rest, write.

I must find a rhythm, to write.

I will find a rhythm, to write.

Soon.

Recovery

Recovery is a gift. It is.

By being sober you connect to your highest Self.

If not, life on this Planet is too harsh. Complicated. Hard.

In recovery, I connect to my feelings. Thoughts. Underlying thoughts, patterns. Beliefs.

I connect to God in order to make it work. Life. Recovery. Love. And other drugs.

I trust. Surrender, see things from, a different perspective.

Awake.

Enlightened.

Free.

God

In God we trust.

And when you do so, life gets a little bit lighter.

You get a little bit lighter.

I get a little bit lighter.

Love.

Dove

"You will when you, believe".

I believe.

I will when I believe.

And so it is.

Work

I return to work.

I do not go home, just yet.

I continue to investigate my future. Past.

Ayahuasca.

Rest.

Repeat.

A rollercoaster.

Life.

Let go, let go, let go. She says. Let go.

Life is one big. Flow.

And so it is.

Write

Is she waking me up in order to write?

She is.

And so it is.

Parents

I'm 31.

I do not need to say, sorry.

But I do.

Please forgive me.

I love you too.

I do.

No

I'd love to learn how to say no.

I need to learn how to say no.

Thank you.

I prefer not to.

See you.

Talk to you.

Be with you.

And so it is.

Maybe

I'm done.

I'm not interested.

Maybe later.

Maybe not.

Why is it so hard to say no?

Yes

I'm learning how to say no.

I'm learning when to say no.

So eventually, I can say yes. Hell yes.

Ready

I'm in.

I got it.

I'm ready.

Will I ever?

No.

Night

I take a shower.

For the first time in 10 days, there's hot water.

And I know, in that moment, that God exists.

If only, you make the right choices. If only, you align with God's will.

God wants us to be happy.

Carefree.

Infinity

Here's what I'm learning.

Things only work out if they're supposed to work out. If they don't, they do not, flow.

If they're hard, complicated, difficult, they're usually not supposed to work, out.

If things are easy, accessible, free, it's usually what's right, for me.

A meeting. Online.

God does not want us to jump off cliffs.

He wants us to make conscious, clear, right-minded decisions.

And so it is.

Morning

I go out.

Calm, centered, awake.

I'm feeling so much better. Did I ever imagine life to be precisely like this?

No. I couldn't ever imagine my life would be this ~~perfect~~.

Imperfect.

Incomplete.

And feeling good, nonetheless.

Feeling calm, conscious, free.

Feminine, strong.

She.

Flow

If you're doing what you're supposed to be doing, life flows.

It is easy. It does not take much, effort.

Effortless.

In Yoga, we move effortlessly, my teacher says.

India. One year ago.

Time flies.

When will I ever?

I will when I believe.

A novel

A miracle.

This is happening.

For real, I'm here.

I'm here, I'm free.

And so it is.

Milagro

I work with Alina.

Money issues. Family issues. Lots of similarities.

We work, tap, talk, try to continue going. And it works.

It works if you work it.

She's feeling so much better.

Whatever I'm doing, works.

I finally reap the benefits of my work.

Every single day, I pray.

> "God grant us the serenity to accept the things we cannot change, the
> courage to change the things we can, and the wisdom to know the
> difference"

Thy will not mine, be done.

Amen.

We have breakfast.

Myriam, Bill. Alina is sitting in front of me. She's kind. Polite, gentle. Whole-hearted.

If only she'd see, what I've seen before.

An angel.

And so it is.

Hero

At the buffet, I meet John. He fuels up. Bigtime.

He joins us for breakfast, shortly.

Then, we say goodbye.

Norway.

Stay.

Food

I eat so much food.

Things I've never eaten before. Eggs, figs. Platano, butter. Ham, cheese. I fuel up.

Bigtime. Watermelon. Tea.

Dessert.

Brownies. Caramel syrup, cake. Pudding.

It's too much but I enjoy it nonetheless. It's delicious.

I fill up every little corner of my body.

A feast.

Boy

I no longer want my tattoo. Boy.

On my back.

Jack

I'm no longer a girl, not yet a woman.

That's what I felt, first.

Then I felt quite masculine, all of a sudden. Change.

I did my first Ayahuasca. Ceremony.

She turned me into a hero, warrior, art.

First.

Fart

Memories fly by.

Seaside, another story. My ex-boyfriend.

We get into a fight. Do not make up. He hurts me, often. Hits me, at times.
Almost.

I lost it. He lost it. We lost it, when we lost our second child. Wild.

Worries.

Why

Cry.

Die

Eventually, I leave.

Him.

Thank God I did, in time.

Rhyme.

Rhythm. Blues.

My baby.

Boy.

Toy

I find God.

A whole new world.

I find God and I remember what I've forgotten before.

I'm enough.

I'm good, I'm gone.

I'm not.

Yet.

Crash

Lots of tears, pain, heart, broken.

Lots of sadness, regret.

I lost my child.

Why do I always hurt myself?

Because I do.

And so do you.

We did.

We did so, together.

And now it's over and there's nothing more to lose, no more.

It's done.

And so it is.

Brussels

I move out, into another apartment.

After a few weeks at home, I return to work.

I'm no longer bleeding, seeing things, I did not see before. I'm sort of stable, clear, calm.

Sort of.

Suicidal.

I think of jumping in front of the subway, often.

But I don't.

Instead, I call my little brother.

My lovely little brother.

"I'm sorry. Please forgive me. I love you. Thank you".

I just didn't dare, to tell my truth.

I felt so hurt, harmed, heartbroken. I felt so damaged, done.

Thank God, it's past.

It's no longer present, times.

I'm better now.

I'm so much better now.

So why would I go there again?

I don't.

I stay.

Right, here, now.

Calm, present. Alive, awake.

Art.

Tropics

It starts raining really heavily in Iquitos. La Casona, my hotel lobby. I'm not sure where I'll sleep, tonight.

All of a sudden I'm not sure of going to Arkana, again. The Amazon.

Maybe I've seen enough, sun, mosquitos, mosh. Maybe I'd like to do, something different.

Do I want to go to Lima after all? See my brother, my mom, my friends?

I do.

Say hi, how do you do?

Connection

I check flight, tickets, online.

Do I or do I not? Go to Lima.

I do.

But not just yet.

Maybe later. When I'm ready.

Will I ever be ready?

No.

Travel

I never thought I'd be a traveler.

But now I am, all of a sudden, a traveler.

I travel way more often than I could ever imagine. Life.

Life's a trip. A fairy tale. A journey.

"A journey", Rodrigo says. My beautiful Brazilian friend. He says it often.

"Every journey is different", he says.

He's right.

And so I continue, my journey.

From Iquitos to Lima, my brother.

I pack my bags, run, wait.

"Soon I'm gonna leave my rags 'n' run".

Will I ever stop running?

Luggage

Wait. There's no rush. Ever.

There's never any rush. It's just life.

If it doesn't feel good, don't.

If it feels good, do.

And so I do.

Not.

Yet.

Almost.

Ghost

Why do I feel so blue?

Clouds

What's my worst fear?

Hurting others.

Disappointing others.

I must make sure I do not hurt, myself.

No more.

I'm feeling better. Calm, bright.

Daylight.

God did not reply, just yet.

I talk to Teo.

Life is changing, every little minute. So why define love, based upon temporary feelings?

Love is a conscious, committed act.

It's not a feeling that you're overwhelmed with.

A Course in Miracles says, "make your romantic relationships more brotherly and your brotherly relationships more romantic".

I've never read anything more right.

It changed my life completely.

What if I take some time off, go to Lima and actually see my parents?

Do not run, hide. Show up.

Do not isolate.

Connection is key. Love.

A mosquito bites my leg.

Do I truly want to return to the jungle?

I'm not sure yet.

Set

LCP Peru

I book my flight. I do not return to Cusco, yet. I'm set.

Why? Why don't I go, home?

Do I want to write, work, play for a living? Giving.

Yes, maybe I do.

And I'd love to be, with you.

Others. Mothers.

Art.

Fifty

My parents are almost sixty.

They're not always right. No more.

They're mostly not right. No more. They're mostly wrong.

Maybe we're both right. Wrong. Maybe we're just, very different.

Maybe we're not meant to spend so much time, together.

Maybe we're just meant to be, free.

Respect each other, let be.

Let be, let be, let be.

Free.

Love

Teo texts me. Again.

He's playing football. I ask him, how he's doing.

Alright, he says. I'm fine.

I wonder how he's really doing.

Will I ever, know?

Does he, know?

He does not. Do so.

And so I go.

Karma

You're so beautiful.

Few hours later.

I run into her, again.

You too.

We drink water from a coconut.

This is love, I think.

My story is not meant to end.

It is meant to continue going.

Why is it so hard to let go?

I don't know.

Diner

One more time. Diner. Together.

Heidi, Denise.

Bill, Myriam.

Myself.

I'm winging it.

Denise starts talking to a stranger. I feel relieved.

So many beautiful compliments.

"You were my favorite go to person".

I blush.

"Can I buy you ice-cream?"

I say yes. God bless.

Lucuma

Culture. Curiosity. Clarity.

Clean.

Word

"Lucuma is a type of fruit native to Peru. Long used as a sweetener and a flavoring agent for foods such as ice cream, lucuma is also said to offer a variety of health benefits. Widely available in powder form, lucuma is often touted as a rich source of nutrients including beta-carotene, vitamin B3, iron, zinc, calcium, magnesium, and other vitamins and minerals. It also contains protein, antioxidants, and dietary fiber."

Cathy Wong

World

Warrior.

What's in a word?

Love.

Dove

And so I continue. Going.

I just know.

I can continue, moving, running. Staying, standing. Still.

At my own pace.

/peɪs/
noun

a single step taken when walking or running.
"Kirov stepped back a pace"

speed in walking, running, or moving.
"he's an aggressive player with plenty of pace"

Write

For a living. Giving.

Focus.

And so it is.

Commitment

I've always traveled plenty. A lot.

But it used to be, a break. From life, work. A holiday.

Now, traveling is what I do for a living. I travel through life. My life is a trip. And I'm enjoying it, so much.

I've never been a big fan of stability. Short term, yes. Long term, no. Go.

I lost it, whenever things got serious. Stable. Concrete.

Commitment.

And I remember.

I wish I didn't but I do, love you.

And you, how do you do?

Fake

I no longer force myself.

To do things, I'm not quite ready for.

To go out, get a tattoo. Jump off cliffs, climb mountains.

I stay still. Grounded.

Pachamama.

And so it is.

Feel

Don't be afraid to catch feels.

Now, I try to feel, first.

I try to feel what's going on within.

Feel what's working, for me. Do not decide, just yet.

I'm set.

I no longer need, a new tattoo. Girl. Friend.

I no longer need, much.

I do need love, kindness. Touch.

Smudge.

Course

One more night.

We go out. Pizza.

It's still raining.

I fly to Lima, tomorrow.

It's done.

All of a sudden I feel unsure.

Unstable.

"Those who are certain of the outcome can afford to wait and wait without anxiety".

So why didn't I wait, longer?

I'm not sure.

Yet.

Jesus

How can I go from full-blown miracle worker to anxious, terrified, trouble maker?

I need a timeout.

I try to distract myself. It's not working.

And so I watch, Netflix, try, TV. I cannot pay attention at all.

I go to bed, wake up, middle of the night.

Is this the aftermath?

Pray

I'm not sure why I pushed myself to get out there. In here.

In my mind, body, Soul. Give in, surrender. To this bigger entity, the Universe. With love.

I now feel so lost, in daily life.

I'm not eating well.

I do not pay attention.

I'm not sure what to do, next.

I know I must make a change but I'm not sure what, exactly.

What must I do, see, say?

I pray.

Universe

Stay.

You've run enough already.

It is time to leave Iquitos, now.

Where do I go?

Brother

I call my brother.

I tell him, I'll be coming home tonight.

I'll stop by, after dinner.

He says, okay.

It's okay.

Stay.

Lima

Few hours later I'm on a flight to Lima.

"I follow rivers".

Lykke Li.

God

Why do I go to Lima?

Art, beauty, bike. Sun, shine, surrender.

A holiday within a holiday, for me. Just for me.

Wouldn't I rather go elsewhere, discover, something new?

No. For now, I just want to be, home.

Recovery

I must put my recovery first.

Calls, outreach. Go to meetings, see friends. Do not isolate, connect.

Recreate.

Miracles.

Let God do the work, for you.

I let God do the work, for me.

All I need to do is sit, watch, wait.

Wonder.

And so it is.

Write

Write. I must write.

I'm doing this, all of this, in order to write.

Recover.

Get better.

I'd love to write my first book, one day.

And until that day, I stay.

Pray

I must learn how to stay somewhere, home.

How to home, for dummies.

Google.

No reply.

God.

And so it is.

Ohm

I must recreate the meaning of home.

I must recreate what it is, was, to be home, come home, for me.

Honestly.

Where is my home?

Ohm

Here. I belong.

Where? There.

Queer.

Culture

I love my classes. Yoga classes.

I miss it so much. Already.

Ten more days of no Yoga but parents, foster, children.

I'm a foster child.

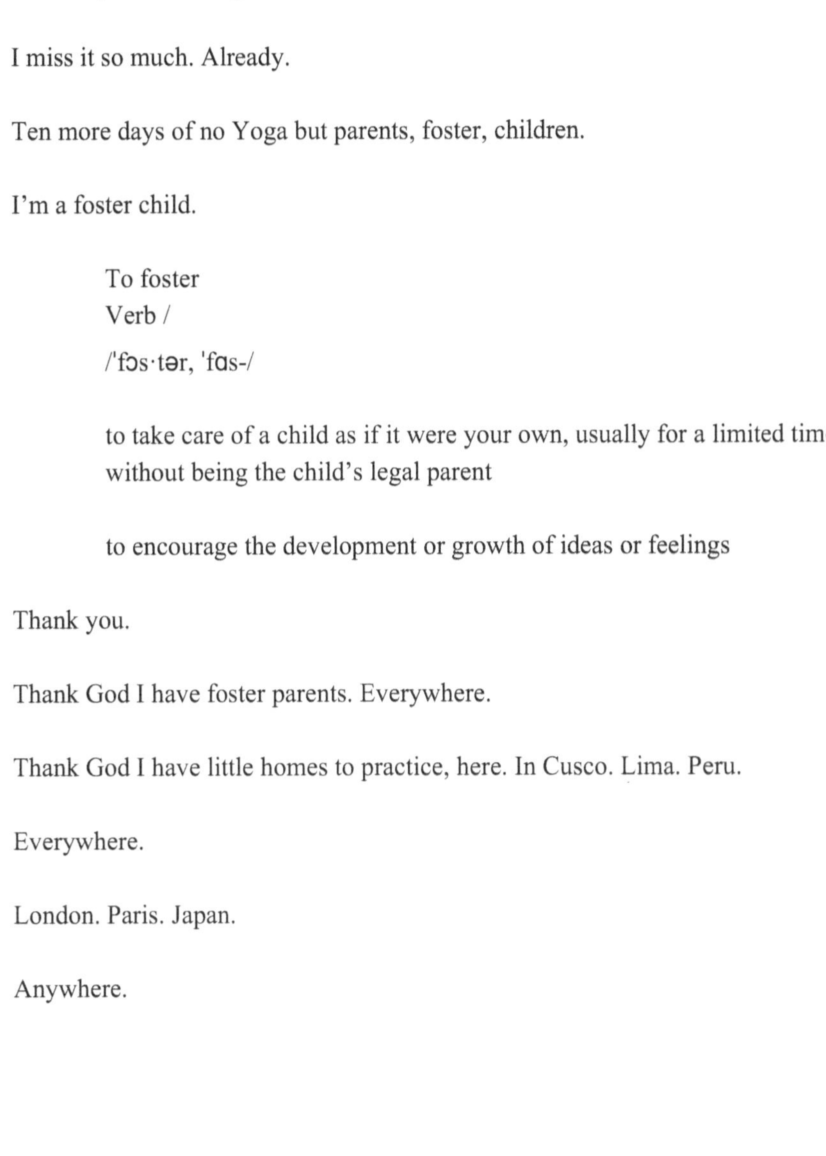

> To foster
> Verb /
> /'fɔs·tər, 'fɑs-/
>
> to take care of a child as if it were your own, usually for a limited time, without being the child's legal parent
>
> to encourage the development or growth of ideas or feelings

Thank you.

Thank God I have foster parents. Everywhere.

Thank God I have little homes to practice, here. In Cusco. Lima. Peru.

Everywhere.

London. Paris. Japan.

Anywhere.

There

I'm sorry.

Please forgive me. I love you.

Thank you.

Hospital

Frida Kahlo.

Mexico.

Teo.

I love you so.

I'm not gay. I'm just terrified of love.

Loving you.

Too.

Girls

I do like girls. Their hair, flair, fun, time out. In. Belonging.

Breasts.

I'm bi.

Queer.

Queen.

Whatever works, will do.

And so do you.

Nike

Don't define, just do.

It.

Time

Is this useful?

Time in, out, my mind.

Headspace.

Mindfulness.

It is, useful.

I improve.

Myself.

And I connect.

To my intuition, my inner Self.

Before you know you'll be a book on a shelf.

Self

Sit. Meditate. Straight.

Magic. Power.

Divine. Feminine.

Energy.

Ritual. Ceremony. Ancestors.

Coming

This trip is becoming everything I ever dreamt of.

Only I didn't know it, yet.

I didn't see it coming, at all. I thought I was here, to do good work.

I'm here, to do better. To do my best.

I'm only getting better.

My best.

And so it is.

Publish

Publish what you write.

It should not be that difficult. It is easy.

There must be a way.

Namastay.

Gold

Old.

You're not growing old, just yet.

Unfold.

Another story, to be told.

London

What do you want?

Stages. Eventually.

For now, just continue, going. Living. Life.

Writing.

Take care of yourself, others.

It is not over yet.

You're not dying. You're alive.

Right here, right now.

You go.

Creativity

A spark.

Future, past.

Present, moment.

Continue to do what you're doing for a living.

Life.

Yoga, arts, writing.

Work.

Whatever works will do.

And so do you.

Steps

Five.

I work my step 5 with my sponsor. It's hard.

I read, pages, resentments. Fears, recovery. Harms, done to myself, others.

The list goes on and on and on.

Will it ever end?

And I forgive. Others.

Myself.

Over and over and over again.

Again.

Time

I need more time to do what I'm doing for a living.

Write.

A better writer.

Work.

A better worker.

Time.

A better timing.

Truth.

A better truth.

Wait. Is there a better truth?

There's not.

There's just life, as we live it and love, as we imagine it to be.

Free.

Alone

A home would make all the difference.

So why don't I look for a home, myself?

I recreate the chaotic patterns I grew up in.

I recreate chaos.

Disorder.

Elements.

I wait. For what's next.

I must direct my life.

I go with God.

Order.

Divine. Order.

I surrender.

I pray.

Stay.

Jessica

My new friend.

Her name is Jessica.

She's beautiful.

I work with her.

She works with me.

We work, together.

It works.

She's a singer. In a band.

We sing.

Karaoke.

Coca-Cola. Sprite.

We try, to do better, every day.

I pray.

Sweden

Jessica.

Where you're at?

Must I come look for you?

Yes.

I feel as if, I do.

Truth

Everything I've written so far, is true.

And you, how do you do?

God

An oracle.

I wait, wish, wonder. What's next?

What to do? Where to go, what to say?

Stay.

Adriana

Eckhart Tolle.

"The Power of Now".

A gift for Adriana, before she left.

Relationships

Mindful relationships.

"We will relate to others from a state of wholeness".

I miss her already.

Life

Eternal flame.

> "Close your eyes, give me your hand, darling
> Do you feel my heart beating
> Do you understand
> Do you feel the same
> Am I only dreaming
> Is this burning an eternal flame"?

Fire. Wind, water. Earth.

Nature.

Elements.

Energy.

Alive

And so I work, my step five.

High five.

I'm alive.

And so it is.

Jessica

Just check, where she, is at.

If not, at least, you tried.

Alright.

Night

I do not find her no more.

She's gone.

Cold

Let life unfold.

Live life, a little. Just live.

Life.

Morning

What to do next?

I'll build. A WordPress. Page.

I'll gather my words.

Somewhere.

Monday

Lines get blurry.

I'm doing Yoga, meditation, art.

Art, writing, Yoga.

Meditation.

Life.

Chore

It is so easy to go to work, get your pay, check, go home, alright.

It is so easy to numb, drink, fade, away.

It is so easy to talk in circles.

As if life is not happening.

No more.

Chore.

Anonymous

It is way more difficult to do things differently.

Your way.

My way.

And so I stay.

<h1 style="text-align:center">Call</h1>

I'm late.

For my meeting.

How can I be late for almost everything?

I'm not sure. I'm just missing out, on life. Why?

God, help me here. Help me surrender.

Help me accept the things I cannot change, give me the courage to change the things I can.

Change.

I'm almost crying.

Almost.

But not, just yet.

I'm set.

Why

Why do I try so hard to live a truthful life?

Why can't I just accept what's right, here now?

Why can't I hide what's not working, shine light on what's right for me?

Because I want to be free.

Peru

What does freedom look like, one might ask.

I'd say, freedom looks like, birds.

Flying high, in the sky.

Clouds, rainbow high.

A fairytale.

Picture perfect, story.

"I'm sorry.

Please forgive me.

I love you.

Thank you".

Today

I'm so done doing.

I'm so done dealing, healing, doing, art. From the heart.

I'm so done trying. To be different, someone new. Someone better, I'm not yet.

There.

Today, I accept.

Who I am, where I'm going.

Today, I accept.

Where I'm at, today.

Today, I accept.

My Self.

Away

All my life I've run away.

I now try to stay.

Stability

I need to stop doing the big things. Move, change, geographicals.

I need to start with little. Things. My job, writing, art.

From the heart.

A fresh start.

Smart.

Sober

I need to sober up, bigtime.

Alarms.

I need to learn how to take care of me. Alone. By myself. Alright.

All is right.

Life is no longer a fight.

Night.

Teo

Few minutes later my mind flies off to Mexico City.

La Condesa.

Rosetta, Roma.

American Apparel. Street style.

Sushi.

Next door, sake.

I return to my energy.

My Self.

Soon I will be a book on a shelf.

Sofia

Teo.

Cuernavaca.

A wedding of far-away friends. Future.

Plans.

We fell in love. Bigtime.

Husband. Wife.

Wifey.

I bought a T-shirt, saying Wifey.

For fun. To play. If only he'd say, "I love you".

Please forgive me.

I'm sorry.

Thank you.

Care

And so I restart.

From the heart.

Art.

Always

Only now I see I was all this time the girl I wanted to be.

All along.

I just didn't see it yet.

The clothes, hair, cut. The cell, phone, ceiling. The songs. Lullaby. Boyfriend.

I've always been who I've wanted to be. Free.

I just didn't see it yet.

I didn't feel it. Yet.

I was too busy pleasing, myself, others.

I was too busy trying to be someone I'm not.

I was too busy judging, analyzing, jeopardizing my future.

Living from the head, not heart.

Living from the mind, not gut.

I was too busy being, doing, seeing straight.

I didn't see the light.

Bright.

Colorful.

A rainbow, maybe.

Free

Falling

In. And out of love.

With you.

Too.